CRACKING
Through My
EGG SHELL

ANGELA J. HOGLE

Cracking Through My Egg Shell: A Memoir

Copyright © 2022 by Angela J. Hogle

Published in the United States of America.

ISBN   Paperback: 978-1-958030-21-9
ISBN   eBook: 978-1-958030-22-6

All rights reserved. No part of this publication may be reproduced, stored in a retrieval system or transmitted in any way by any means, electronic, mechanical, photocopy, recording or otherwise without the prior permission of the author except as provided by USA copyright law.

The opinions expressed by the author are not necessarily those of ReadersMagnet, LLC.

ReadersMagnet, LLC
10620 Treena Street, Suite 230 | San Diego, California, 92131 USA
1.619.354.2643 | www.readersmagnet.com

Book design copyright © 2022 by ReadersMagnet, LLC. All rights reserved.
Cover design by Ericka Obando
Interior design by Daniel Lopez

Dedication

To my wonderful parents who always supported me

Also to my husband who gave me great support in this adventure of writing a book

Last but not least, to my son who gives me so much joy each day.

Angela J. Hogle

CRACKING *Through My* EGG SHELL

My story of cracking through my shell started a long time ago when I was in second grade. I will not tell you what year that was. That was the time I diagnosed with what is called Turner Syndrome.

Turner is something that happens to girls. Basically, a short explanation is we are missing a chromosome. There are many things that can come with having Turner. You can have liver problems, problems with your kidneys and heart problems.

At the time I was diagnosed they knew about Turner but were trying to learn more about it. I remember one time when I had to go for a twelve-hour blood test. They needed to put an IV in my arm. I was terrified of needles. They could not find a vein. I ended up becoming a human pin cushion. I was screaming because of all the poking they ended up doing on me.

A few years later I would be put on growth hormone to help my body get to my maximum height which met a shot every day. I had such a wonderful mother who gave them to me each day. I did eventually get up enough nerve to give them to myself. I also had to go to a hospital a few times to get a check up and get my height checked. I remember the time we went, they checked my height as they normally did. The nurse came in, and I could tell she had a different look on her face. Well, she said, it looks like you are done growing. They did an x-ray to make sure they did not see any more room for growth. They did not see any more room in the bones for growth. I was four feet nine inches and I was done growing. At this time, I was getting close to the teenage years. I was probably around 11 years old. The idea of being only four foot bothered me. Here I was at the age I was thinking about dating but who was I. I was to different. In my mind I thought that no guy is going to look at me and see me for who I was. They would see a little girl. I would never be a 5'9" model. Those were the years where being in the CLUB was everything. I started to get a very bad self-esteem. I did not have a lot of friends mostly because I was thinking people looked at me different. One thing my parents tried to engrain in me was that God never says **"OOPS!"** God made each of us special. Psalms 139:13 says *"You Knitted me together in my mother's womb"*. Now I do not knit but I do some crocheting. When I read this verse I picture Him carefully weaving together all of intricate pieces to make a wonderful masterpiece. If you do any sewing or knitting you know the joy you feel when you look and admire your finished project. When I work on a project I have to tear out mistakes many times. God NEVER has to do that. He makes no mistakes when He forms us and He has a purpose for each and every one of our lives. I reached my senior year of high school. I was trying to figure out where God was leading me.

I graduated high school and went off to college. I went to Heritage Baptist University in Indiana. The school was not far from where my sister and her family lived. I was excited to get to visit them on the weekends. I met a guy there. I only went out with him because I was afraid no one else would come along. I finally made the wise decision and broke off our relationship. I graduated with an associate degree. I still wanted to meet my prince charming but after the breakup I kind of put it out of my mind. I did not realize what was ahead of me. I am reminded of the story of Joseph. He was put through so much. He did not know what God was doing in his life. IN the end he saw God's hand in everything. God eventually moved me to Ohio to teach Kindergarten at a Christian school. It was there I met my wonderful husband. Our church had a singles group. We would get together on Sunday nights. We had a Christmas gathering one year. That was the first time I noticed my husband. One night after our singles group I was headed to my car. He drove his truck over to where I was. He asked me out and the rest they say is history. We were married on September 25, 1999. After being married for two years our journey began to start a family. We started with trying in vitro using a donated egg. We were devastated when that failed. Through the years we had opportunities to adopt but they did not work out. I was beginning to wonder if God cared. He knew the desire of my heart. Psalms 37:4-5 says *"Delight thyself also in the Lord, and He shall give thee the desire of thine heart. ⁵Commit thy way unto the Lord, trust also in Him: and He shall bring it to pass."* I kept thinking God, you said you would give us the desire of our hearts. Satan used this to tell me lies that God did not care. I fought those thoughts day after day. Satan knows where we are weak. For me, it was my infertility. What is it in your life? Maybe its finances. You have a hard time when you struggle to make ends meet. You think if God loves you He would not let you struggle financially, whatever it is in your life, we need to fight those feelings and give them to God. Matthew 11:29 says," Take *my yoke upon you, and learn of me for I am meek and lowly in heart: and ye shall find rest unto your soul."*

I guess you could say that the first try was the start of me cracking through my shell. God was beginning to work in my life.

A few years later I was volunteering at a place called Hannah's home. It is a place for teenage pregnant girls. One of the girls came to me and asked if my husband and I would like to adopt her baby. We started to get to know each other. We would go shopping she came to see our home. Everything looked like we would be adopting the baby. Some time passed and she decided to keep the baby. That was more struggle cracking through the egg shell. We went on with our lives. We did not try anything. It was not that I did not want to have a child but I was trying to be contented without a family.

One of the hardest times for me was on Mother's Day. Every year I would cry and cry. We went to a small church. Most of the married women all had family. There was one older lady, her name was Mrs. B. She and her husband never had children. We had many talks. When Mother's day came I would be up in the choir and I would look for her. She was my encouragement to get through the day. I remembered her telling me one time that she would not come to church on Mother's day except that she knew I needed encouragement. Even at her age, Mother's day was still hard for her. We both had to lean on the Lord for strength. I thank the Lord for putting her in my life. God sends people into our lives to walk along side of us to encourage us through tough times in our lives. I was trying to have the right attitude but I was getting bitter towards God. I would look at these women with families and think *"Why are you doing this God?"*.

Does that ever happen to you? Maybe you lost a loved one and you start getting bitter toward God for taking them. Satan uses those times to put thoughts in your mind. Thought that God does not love you or He would not have allowed a certain circumstance happen. That is how Satan works. Look at the Garden of Eden with Eve. He put lies into her head. He told her God did not want them to eat the fruit because then they would be like God. That was false. Eve believed the lie and ended up eating the fruit that God told them not to eat and they had to suffer the consequences. That is what we do so many times, don't we?

We think we know what is best. Just because we want something we move in a direction we should not go. Maybe it is with a job. There is a job that pays a lot more than what you are getting. You only take the job because you see the extra money. You know it is not where God wants you. You end up being miserable because even with the extra money you are out of the will of God. I fought that feeling all the time. I kept telling God I would try to be happy without children because I wanted to be in the will of God. To try and help the empty feeling, I helped with our local county Friends for Life. I enjoyed helping in our table during our county fair. I will never forget the time a young man stopped and was looking at our table. We had a display of each stage the baby goes through in the womb. He looked at me and said, *"You mean they are not just a blob?"* It was wonderful to get to share with him and many others how precious life is. Things were going well. I was feeling better about things. I had a job I really enjoyed. I was a in home caregiver for elderly. Then some things changed. My husband's sister had gotten married and now a couple years later had announced she was going to have a baby. I told her how happy I was for her, I tried to put on a smile. On the inside my heart was breaking.

I was trying to put on a good front.

The day her baby was born my husband was working so I had to go visit her and the baby at the hospital by myself. That was one of the hardest things I have ever done. Sometimes God asked us to do something hard. He is using that situation to help us grow in Him. Look at Abraham in the Bible. He was asked to sacrifice his only son. God wanted to see how strong Abraham's faith was. Abraham trusted God and followed God's command. It was not until he was ready to sacrifice Isaac that God told him to stop. We know the story but Abraham did not. Could you imagine how hard it must have been for Abraham?

A few years past and both my husband and I had come to terms with the fact God just did not want us to have children. During those years we became very busy on the farm. We planted a lot of produce to sell at a farmer's market. Our big seller was sweetcorn. We were at a farmer's market on Saturday selling our produce when we saw some friends of ours. The lady came up to me and said she wanted to talk to me. We went off to the side to talk. She proceeded to tell me that her son worked with a girl who was pregnant but she did not want to keep the baby. She said that they thought of us right away. I started to get butterflies in my stomach. Could this be happening? Maybe God was opening up a door for us to finally have a family. Later that day I told my husband about what she had told me. We talked about what we should do. Did we really want to try this? At this time, we had been married for fourteen years. We thought God had said no to having children.

We prayed about it and decided that God had opened the door so we should go through the door until He closes the door. I am sure you have been in that same place in your own life. You just are not sure if you should make a certain move or not. James 1:5 says," *If any of you lack wisdom let him ask of God that giveth to all men liberally, and upbraided not; and it shall be given him."* The first part of verse 6 says" But *let him ask in faith, nothing wavering"* which means we need to pray with confidence. That is hard for us to do. We need to pray knowing that He will give us what we are asking for if that is best for us. If it is not the best, we must be confident that His ways are better than our ways. Isaiah 55:8 says,

"For my thoughts are not your thoughts, neither are your ways my ways, saith the Lord." The bottom line is we must have confidence that whatever He allows is the best for us. We believed God opened up this door to adopt and wanted us to walk through that door.

My friend told me that the girl had agreed to meet with us. She gave me the girl's number. We set up a time to meet at our local McDonalds. The day came I was nervous about what she would think of us. We had an excellent talk that day and her and her boyfriend decided they wanted us to adopt the baby. She kept in contact with me. She would let me know how her doctor appointments went. As she got farther along, I got a text from her telling me she started to feel the baby move. That started to make me nervous. I knew that that was a bonding time for the mom. I prayed *"Lord, please do not let her get attached to this baby."* She would assure me that the baby was ours. The time came she was to deliver the baby. We went to the hospital. We had our lawyer draw up some papers that stated the baby was to go into our care after birth. The birth mom and the boyfriend both signed the papers. She gave birth to a beautiful baby girl. After she was born, the boyfriend told us that she would be staying with them in their room.

My heart dropped to the floor. *"Here we go."*, I thought. My husband and I went to the room that the hospital let us stay in for the night. I burst into tears and started screaming *"We are going to lose her!"*. After some time, I went over to their room and knocked on the door. I went in and just told her if she had changed her mind she better tells us right now and not lead us on. She assured me that Brooke, that is the name we chose for her, was ours and she had not changed her mind. That evening something wonderful happened. A nurse came in our room and she brought Brooke with her. She said that we would get to have her through the night. Our hearts were rejoicing. What a roller coaster of emotions we had been on so far. We spent that evening bonding with her. I will never forget the image of my husband sitting in the chair with her singing Jesus Loves Me. The next morning something tragic happened. The hospital social workers came into our room. They told us that the papers that we had our lawyer draw up were not legal enough so they could not let us take the baby. This really turned the birth mom's mind around. She told us she was not sure what she was going to do. She told us she might go through an agency. The social workers told us she wanted us to leave the hospital. We left with heavy hearts. I knew it was over but my husband tried to convince me that everything was going to work out and we would get to keep our precious little girl.

The next day I got a text from the birth mom. They were keeping the baby. We were DEVASTATED. How could this be happening again?

There was something else that is going on at the time that make things even harder to deal with. Do you remember my sister-in-law I wrote about earlier? The same time we begin the adoption process, with the birth mom, my sister-in-law announced she was expecting another baby. This meant that she and the birth mom were due at the same time. My sister-in-law had her baby, a baby girl. A couple weeks before the birth mom gave birth to Brooklyn. So not only did we lose Brooklyn, I had a niece the same age that would constantly remind me of the baby girl we lost. When I held my niece, when she was born, I was so excited. In just a couple weeks, I was going to be holding our little girl in my arms. Oh how things changed! It was a couple weeks before I could be around my niece. Even when I did see her, all I can see is Brooklyn's face.

We had prayed about this and felt this was God's leading. Now He had allowed this to happen. Was this Gods will for us from the beginning? Yes, it was. It did not turn out how we thought it should but it was still His will. You see, my husband and I grew so much in our walk with God through this experience. We grew in ways we probably would not have grown if we did not go through this ordeal. Jeremiah 29:11 says *"For I know the thoughts that I think toward you saith the Lord, thoughts of peace and not of evil, to give you an expected end."* In other words, He has our lives planned out from the start. Everything that happens is for a purpose. He knew we needed to go through this hard time to grow us closer to Him. I am sure you have had those times in your life. You went a certain direction thinking for sure it was what God wanted and then it did not turn out the way you thought. It maybe that God is trying to draw you closer to Him. That goes back to the title of the book *"Cracking Through My Egg Shell."*

He has to take us through the struggle of cracking through the shell to mold us and make us into His likeness. The one thing I have learned about hatching chickens is that God gives them what is called an egg tooth. He gives them this tooth to be able to crack through the shell of the egg. After they are done hatching the tooth dissolves. Just like God gives them that egg tooth. He gives us what we need to go through those hard times. In 1 Corinthians 10:13 it says *"There hath no temptation taken you but such as is common to man: but God is faithful, who will not suffer you to be tempted above that ye are able; but will with the temptation also make a way of escape, that ye may be able to bear it."* In so many words, He will give you your egg tooth to go through your struggle. He does not leave us without help when going through hard times.

So the birth mom had changed her mind and my husband and I come home to an empty nursery. I could not walk in the room for a very long time. My husband and I had a decision to make. Do we get rid of all the baby stuff and quit trying to have a family or do we keep trying? I had heard about something called embryo adoption but we had not really look into it. After much prayer we decided God was not done with us yet. There was a reason we had all of the baby stuff. We made the decision to look into embryo adoption. Psalms 16:11 says *"Thou wilt shew me the path of life: in thy presence is fulness of joy; at thy right hand there are pleasures for evermore."* We decided to look into embryo adoption. The first thing we had to do was set up an appointment with the doctor for a physical exam. They need to make sure you are physically able to carry a pregnancy. We were thrilled when I was cleared for a pregnancy. The next step was to get everything done for our home study. That took a few months. After our home study was done you are given a list of donors. You are given all the information like hair color, eye color plus all their medical history. My husband and I decided on a donor. The time finally came to go to Tennessee where the clinic was located and have a transfer done.

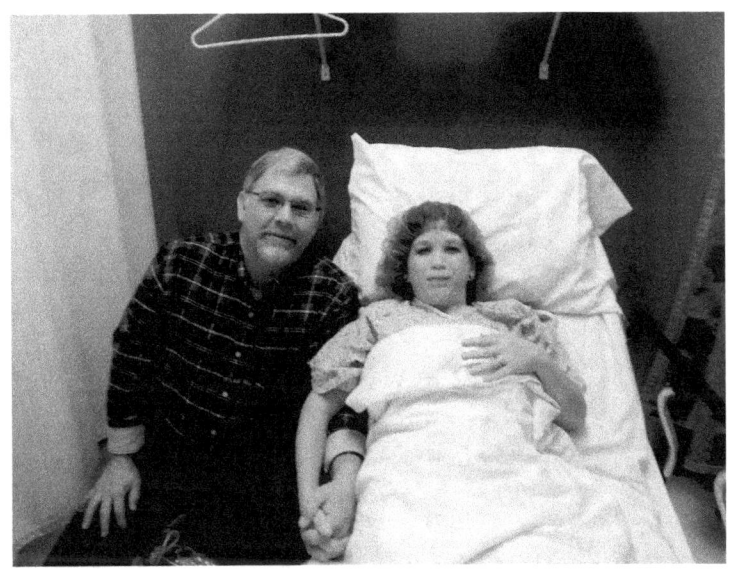

Getting ready for the transfer! I was so nervous!

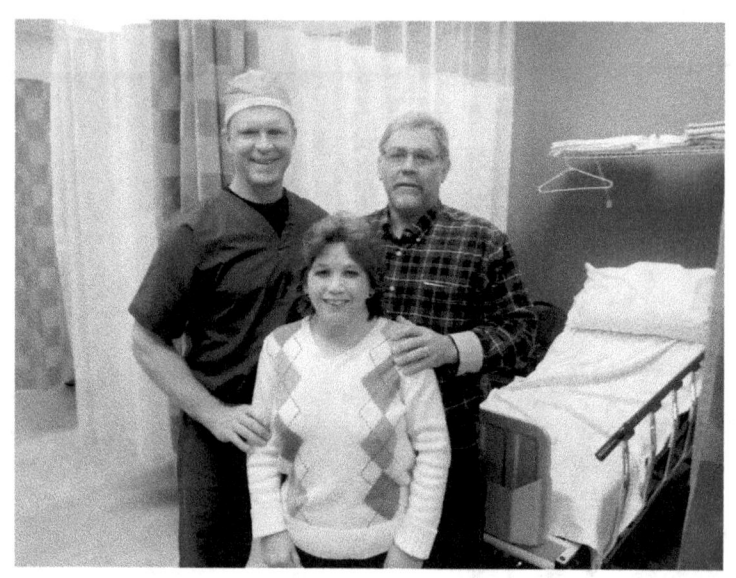

My husband and I with the doctor who did the transfer.

After the transfer you have to wait two weeks for a pregnancy test. Those were the longest 2 weeks of my life. We were devastated when we got the call from the nurse saying that I was not pregnant. We talked to the doctor a couple of days after we got the news. He told us he could not readily see the reason that it did not work. My levels were great, we had two great embryos. He told us he did not see any reason why could not try another transfer. We were not sure if God wanted us to try again. The way they had to set their schedule they needed to know within just 2 days if we wanted to be on the next transfer cycle. We decided that if they gave us some more time to pray about it and there was an opening we would try one more time. When I called the nurse she said we could have some more time. I then asked if they had an opening in the next transfer cycle. The nurse told me they had a cancellation and they had ONE opening. We decided God was leading us to try again. We had our first transfer done in September. They did transfer every other month. So in November we went down for another transfer. The waiting game started again. Again the two weeks crept by so slow. The time came to take the pregnancy test. I went for the blood test and waited for the nurse to call. The day came to hear. I saw the number of the clinic on my phone. I began to shake uncontrollably. This was it! If it did not work this time we were done trying. I softly said hello. The nurse on the other end said, *"I have some news for you. The test was positive."* I could not believe what I was hearing. This had to be a dream. We were pregnant. After sixteen years of waiting God had answered our prayer. Then Satan began to plant seeds in my mind again. I started to fear that I would have a miscarriage. I have to tell you honestly I lived in fear most of the pregnancy. I was very fearful during the first trimester. As I got further along I got to feel the baby kick. That was such a wonderful feeling. I never thought I would get to feel a precious life growing inside me. As I got even further along and our bundle of joy began to really grow I started to feel the movements less and less. This scared me a lot. The fact was with me not being very big the baby just did not have a whole lot of room to move. I really had to put my faith in God that He would protect our bundle of joy. As far as morning sickness or having toxemia everything went great. I had a great pregnancy. Because of the Turners they were concerned about my heart. They kept a close eye on me during the pregnancy. I did not have ANY problems. They did not want me to go into labor. Labor would put too much strain on my heart. Because of this a C-section was scheduled. In August of 2015, I gave birth to a healthy baby boy. We are so thankful for the healthy child God gave us. He has given us so much joy. This proves God knows what is best for us. At the time, we thought that the adoption was what God wanted. Little did we know at the time He had something so much better for us.

Angela J. Hogle

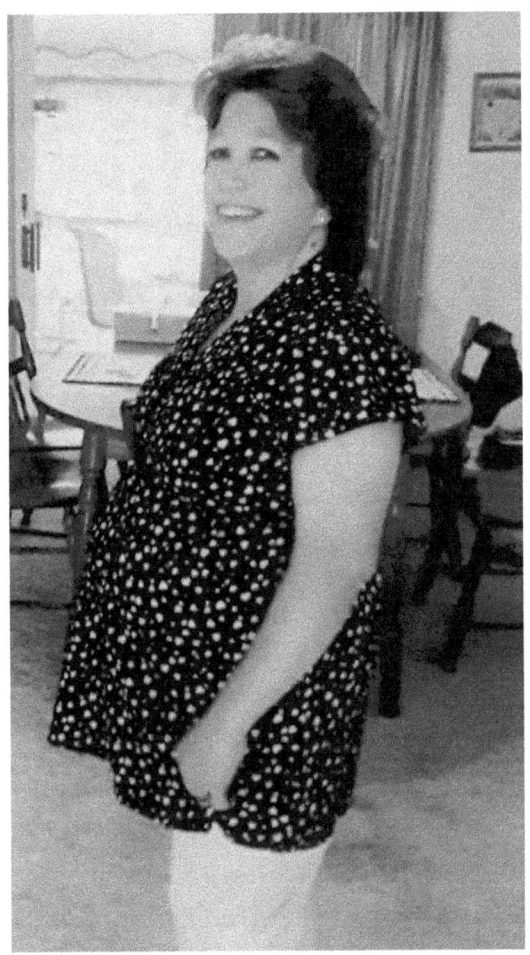

*2 weeks before the C-section.
We were getting so excited!*

CRACKING *Through My* EGG SHELL

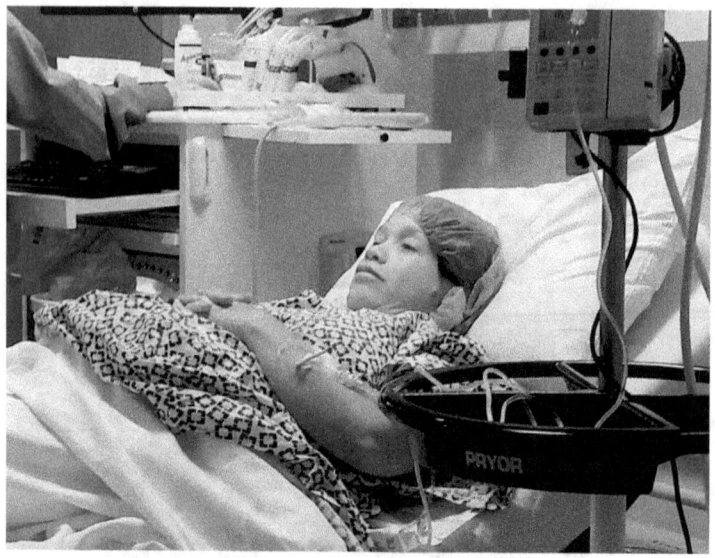

*Ready to go in for the C- section.
Excited and nervous to meet our bundle of joy.*

So the day came for our baby boy to be born. I was so nervous. I have never been one for needles. With having a C-section, I would have to have an epidural A needle in my back. I was scared to death. To make matters worse my C-section was not scheduled until 3:00 In the afternoon. I had all morning to fret and that is exactly what I did.

It was finally time to have the baby and they took me back to get me prepped. My husband could not go back until I was prepped and the divider was in place, he finally came in. Back when we had our checkups my husband told the doctor that he wanted to be able to watch everything. He told the doctor he lived on a farm and nothing bothered him. So when he got in the room he kept trying to look over the divider. The nurses kept yelling at him to sit down. Fortunately, he did not faint. It seemed like in no time I was hearing the cry of our baby boy. That cry was the most beautiful sound in the world. He ended up swallowing some meconium. They had to take him to NICU to help him breathe. My heart dropped. I was scared something might happen. He ended up bouncing back quickly. They would not let him stay in my room. I had to get my heart checked out before they would bring him in my room. At around 4 am in the morning they wheeled me to see him. I was so exhausted but there are no words to describe how I felt when they handed me my baby boy. A 16-year prayer had been answered.

They eventually brought him to my room. Then another hurdle came. He did not want to nurse. He was bottle fed in the NICU and that is what he wanted. There were many stressful hours trying to get him to nurse but to no avail. He wanted the bottle. The day came to take him home. Fear overwhelmed me again. We were now totally responsible for this little life. Sure, I had done lots of babysitting in my days but this was different. This was my own child. I had to do a lot of praying that God would give us wisdom. I had to realize there are no perfect parents we would make mistakes all parents make mistakes. I have felt the feeling of inadequacy many times. I felt like such a failure as a parent. Phillipians 4:13 says, "I can do all things through Christ who strengthens me. I cannot parent on my own. I have to constantly go to God for guidance".

I remember sitting in the car in the hospital parking lot ready to take our son home both of us began to cry. We were so grateful for the miracle God did for us. My mind flashed backed to all we had been through, all the hard times we had to endure. How many times we forget that God sees our beginning to our end. He sees the whole picture.

Last summer we took a trip to Pigeon Forge Tennessee. They have the Island there with different rides and games and shops. One of the rides is a big Ferris wheel. You sit in an enclosed compartment. Jake, our boy, was not real excited about riding it. Once we got in and started going he had a blast. He loved looking out and seeing for miles. That is the way God sees our life. He sees everything at one time. We see our lives just a little bit at a time. It is not until we have gone through the valley that we look back and see Gods purpose. Sometime he shows us right away sometime it may take a while and sometimes we may never know His purpose until we reach heaven.

Being a mother was going to be different then I had imagined. When I finally got pregnant we decided that I would be a stay at home mom. I thought I would enjoy staying at home. Do not get wrong, I enjoy every moment I get to spend with my son. When he was around 2 I began to think I needed to get involved with something. I had heard about some other moms I knew going to a MOPS group. This stands for mothers of preschoolers. I started to look for one around my area. I found one and joined. I would encourage any mother out there whether you are a stay at home mom or a working mom to find a MOPS close to you and get involved. It is a group of moms that help support each other in the journey of being a mother. They go on outings together. They help out different organizations. Going to MOPS helped but I was still fighting to find my identity. I had worked since I was 16 years old up until I had my son. My husband had the farm. He and his dad did most of that work. His mom was in charge of the finances. The question was, where did I belong. I became very inward. I felt I had no worth anymore. In Matthew 10:31 it says," fear not, therefore, you are of more value than many sparrows". I had to come to realize that my identity did not come from my husband or anyone else. My Identity comes from God. I am loved by God like I could ever be loved by someone here on earth and so are you. We need to stop looking at those around us and concentrate on who we are to God.

Remember I was a city girl. I knew nothing about country life and all of a sudden I was put in, what seemed to me. a foreign world. To me a cow was a cow, I would soon learn different when I got into my husband's family. A couple years after we were married my husband and I got some chickens. This would be my first go at trying to be "a farmer". The time came to butcher the chickens. My husband handed me the ax to chop the head. I could not believe I was doing it but I took a deep breath and gave a swing. I guess that was my initiation into farm life. In another few years we would get goats. That was another experience. We bred the goats to have their baby in winter. So that met getting up at all hours and taking a Long walk in the deep snow down to the barn to check if any of them were kidding. This was all new for this city girl. There were a few times for various reasons I would have to bottle feed one of the babies. So again, getting up during the night to feed the baby. This was all a new experience to me. There was a time one of the goats was having trouble during birth. We called the vet. My husband had to go to work so I assisted the vet in preforming a C-section. There were so many things to get used to in country life but I began to love it and I would not change a thing. I love the fact we get to rear our boy on the farm and boy does he love it.

Many times God will take us out of our comfort zone to teach us things and help us grow. I know I have learned a lot about myself living on the farm. Its that idea of Cracking Through the Egg shell again. He puts us in what we feel are uncomfortable situations. When that chicken is ready to hatch it is very uncomfortable it does not have much room in that shell. If life were always easy for us we would never learn and grow to be what God wants us to be.

Another area of farm life I was not used to was how busy life gets especially during the summer and even fall. I have a husband Who works 24/ 7. He works on the farm and also has a third shift job. When I was growing up I saw my parents doing things together all the time. They would play racquetball together or go on walks together. This, I would soon find out, would not be my life. If you have ever heard of Gary Chapman, he has a book out called "The Five Love Languages". One of the Love Languages is Time. I am one that likes that one on one time. Unfortunately, that could not happen with us. Farm life is a very hectic life. Remember when I talked about being content and not look at other people? That has been my goal. I tend to look at Facebook or Twitter and see everyone going on vacation together or doing some other activity and I get jealous. I have had to learn God has me where I am for a reason and I need to be content. This, I must say, is a constant struggle. I must realize that God is my fulfilment. I should not try and find fulfilment in my relationship with my husband, friends or family. God is the only one that can give true satisfaction. My first priority must be my relationship with God. When that relationship is where it should be the others will fall in line.

I have learned a lot living on the farm things I know I would never have learned if I would have stayed a city girl. We will all go through "Cracking Through the Shell" times in our life. The important thing is when those times come to keep our eyes on the Lord. Know that He has a reason for everything he sends in our life. His plan for our life is always best. Would I have wanted to have Turner syndrome? Of course not but God has used it to teach me so many things. I am so thankful for all He has taught me in my life and the blessing of our son that seemed an impossibility but as Luke 1:37 says "For with God nothing shall be impossible.

CRACKING *Through My* EGG SHELL

If you would have told me I would marry a farmer, I would have told you that you were crazy. I was a city girl. I have learned so much from watching the different animals on the farm. I started learning about chickens so that I could hatch some chicks with my kindergarten class. It always amazed me about the egg tooth, how that it is only there for a short time. It is there just to help the chick crack through the shell. It also amazed me how that if you try to help the chick in any way while it is trying to crack through the shell it will die. This is so much how God works with us. He gives us what we need to go through hard times we have. Those hard times He gives us is to make us stronger. Just like the chick must go through the struggle of hatching through the shell to make it stronger we must go through struggles to make us stronger spiritually.

A song my son loves to sing is "Trust and Obey". It is a familiar song with so much meaning. "Trust and obey for there's no other way to be happy in Jesus but to trust and obey. All He ask us to do is trust Him and obey Him." Like the song says if we do that, we will be happy in Him. Putting our trust in Him is never easy but is truly the only way we can have true joy even in hard times. There is another song I love from the group Greater Vision. The song is called "The Source of My Song". One of the verses says *"If we only sing when were happy, we will not be singing very long. But if were singing while the battles raging, the world will know that Jesus is source of our song."* The chorus says, *"Oh the source of my joy is the Savior. The reason for my singing is this man from Galilee. It does not depend upon my circumstances for Jesus is source of my joy."*

In John 9 there is a story of a blind man. Jesus and His disciples were passing by. In so many words the disciples asked Jesus what horrible thing did the blind man do or his parents for him to be blind. They thought for sure someone must have done something horrible for him to be blind. Jesus shocked them by saying it was not because of anything they had done. It was so that God would be glorified. He then proceeded to spit on the ground and make clay from the dirt and put it on the blind man's eyes and then told him to go wash and he was healed. God was glorified through the man's blindness. When people saw that he was healed he shared his story with others how God had healed him.

    I remember after the adoption fell through, I had a meeting with the boss of the company I was working for. I had quit the job thinking I would be staying at home with the baby. We had a meeting to discuss the possibility of me coming back to work. In our discussion I was able to share my faith and how I believed God was in control. It was such a privilege to get share Christ with her. She did not accept Christ that day but I truly believe a seed was planted. I had another opportunity to share Christ. A friend of mine had given me something for the baby. When the adoption fell through I returned what she had given me. The day I went to her house to return what she had given me we had a great talk. I was able to share my faith with her. There is no doubt God was glorified through that trail.

CRACKING *Through My* EGG SHELL

I would like to share a story of a young lady I know. She attends the church where my husband and I attend, her name is Whitney. Years ago she started to go blind. It was very gradual. Now she is completely blind. She could have stayed home and felt sorry for herself. That is not what she is doing. She has such a sweet spirit. She has decided she wants to be a teacher for children with special needs. She has spent MONTHS getting familiar with the college campus where she wants to attend. She is determined to live on campus. She has not let her blindness stop her one bit. I know for a fact that her life has been a testimony for Christ. People look at her and wonder how she could be so happy with what has happened to her. She has definitely let the joy of Jesus shine through her. I know she has had her down days but she does not let those feelings control her. I hope we can all be that way when trials come into our lives. I hope we can keep in mind that God has a purpose for everything that happens to us good and bad. So I hope if you live in the country and see chickens all the time or if you live in city and visit a place with chickens you will think of how God takes care of those chickens and gives them what they need to get through that shell God will also give us what we need to go through those hard times that will come our way. Matthew 10:29-31 *"29Are not two sparrows sold for a farthing? and one of them shall not fall on the ground without your Father. 30But the very hairs of your head are numbered. 31Fear ye not therefore ye are more valuable than many sparrows."*

God loves us beyond what we could even imagine. He loved us so much He sent his only Son to die for us. If you have accepted Christ we need to have the confidence that God is in charge of our lives and we can go to him for strength through hard times. If you have not accepted Christ, you do not have Him to lean on for strength. My prayer for you is that you will accept Him as your Lord and Savior. All you need to do is admit you are a sinner and you believe He came to die on the cross for your sins and you believe He rose from the dead and ask Him to come live in your heart. If you accept Him, He will be there to carry you through those hard times and give you the strength you need.

Angela J. Hogle

I end with one of my favorite poems called "Footprints".
One-night man had a dream.
He dreamed he was walking along the beach with the Lord.
Across the sky flashed scenes from his life.
For each scene he noticed two sets of footprints in the sand,
one belonged to him and the other to the Lord.
When the last scene of his life flashed before him,
he looked back at the footprints in the sand.
He noticed that many times along the path of his
life there was only one set of footprints.
He also noticed that it happened at the very
lowest and saddest times in his life.
This really bothered him, and he questioned the Lord about it.
"Lord, you said that once I decided to follow You,
You'd walk with me all the way.
But I have noticed that during the most
troublesome times in my life,
there is only one set of footprints.
I don't understand why when I needed
you most you would leave me.
The Lord replied. "My precious, precious child I love you
and I would never leave you.
During your times of trial and suffering
when you see only one set of footprints,
it was then that I carried you".

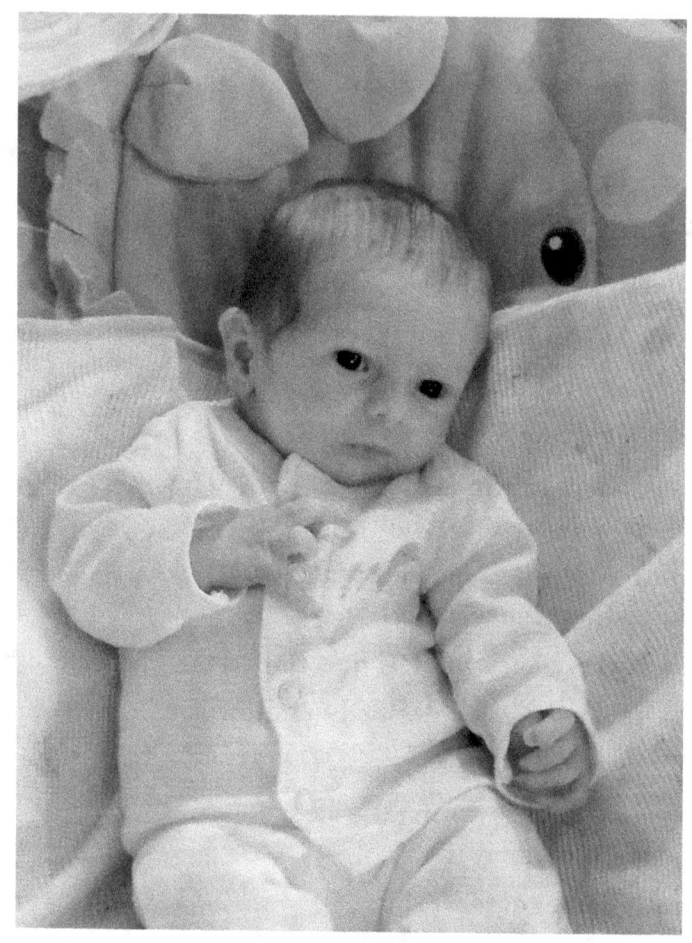

Our little miracle a couple days after we brought him home from the hospital.

www.ingramcontent.com/pod-product-compliance
Lightning Source LLC
LaVergne TN
LVHW021051100526
838202LV00082B/5454